W9-AZU-132

CHAMPIONSHIP TEAMS

i love this game!

SCHOLASTIC INC.

New York   Toronto   London   Auckland
Sydney   Mexico City   New Delhi   Hong Kong

Photos:

Front cover: © by Andrew D. Bernstein/NBAE via Getty Images

Back cover: (left) © Nathaniel S. Butler/NBAE via Getty Images; (middle) © Noren Trotman/NBAE via Getty Images; (right) © Jed Jacobsohn/Getty Images

Interior: (Title page clockwise from top left) © Dick Raphael/NBAE via Getty Images; © NBA Photos Library/NBAE via Getty Images; © Andrew D. Bernstein/NBAE via Getty Images; © Andy Hayt/NBAE via Getty Images
(4, 15 right, 18 bottom, 19 right) © Andrew D. Bernstein/NBAE via Getty Images; (5, 8, 10 middle) © NBA Photos/NBAE/Getty Images; (6 top right, 13 bottom left) © Richard Mackson/ Sports Illustrated/Getty Images; (6 top left) © NBA Photos Library/NBAE via Getty Images; (6 bottom, 12, 23, 25, 26, 30 bottom right) © Dick Raphael/NBAE via Getty Images; (7 left) © Ronald Martinez/ Getty Images; (10 top left) © Rich Clarkson/Sports Illustrated/Getty Images; (10 bottom) © Richard Meek/Sports Illustrated/Getty Images; (10 top right) © Fred Kaplan/Sports Illustrated/Getty Images; (13 top left & bottom right) © Manny Millan/Sports Illustrated/Getty Images; (13 top right) © Getty Images; (14 bottom) © Alexander Hassenstein/Bongarts/Getty Images; (14 top, 17, 18 top, 30 top left) © Nathaniel S. Butler/NBAE via Getty Images; (15 left) © Focus on Sport/Getty Images; (16 left) © AFP/AFP/Getty Images; (16 right, 17 inset) © Noren Trotman/NBAE/Getty Images; (19 left) © Jesse D. Garrabrant/NBAE via Getty Images; (21) © Walter Iooss Jr./Sports Illustrated/Getty Images; (27) © Scott Winterton/NBAE via Getty Images; (29) © John W. McDonough/Sports Illustrated/Getty Images; (30 top right) © Neil Liefer/NBAE via Getty Images; (30 bottom left) © DON EMMERT/AFP/Getty Images

No part of this work may be reproduced, stored in a retrieval system, or transmitted in any form or by any means, electronic, mechanical, photocopying, recording, or otherwise without written permission of the publisher. For information regarding permission, write to Scholastic Inc., Attention: Permissions Department, 557 Broadway, New York, NY 10012.

ISBN 978-0-545-20649-5

The NBA and individual NBA member team identifications, photographs, and other content used on or in this publication are trademarks, copyrighted designs, and other forms of intellectual property of NBA Properties, Inc., and the respective NBA member teams and may not be used, in whole or part, without the prior written consent of NBA Properties, Inc. All rights reserved.

Copyright © 2010 by NBA Properties, Inc.

All rights reserved. Published by Scholastic Inc. SCHOLASTIC and associated logos are trademarks and/or registered trademarks of Scholastic Inc.

12 11 10 9 8 7 6 5 4 3 2 1   10 11 12 13 14 15/0

Designed by Cheung Tai
Printed in the U.S.A.
First printing, January 2010

CONTENTS

CHAPTER 1 . . . . **4**

NBA CHAMPIONS

CHAPTER 2 . . . . **6**

DYNASTIES

CHAPTER 3 . . . . **20**

GREAT CHAMPIONSHIP GAMES

CHAPTER 4 30

NBA CHAMPIONS (YEAR BY YEAR)

CHAPTER 1

NBA CHAMPIONS

Who's Number One? That is the question asked at NBA training camps every October. Thirty NBA teams open camp with one goal in mind — winning the *Larry O'Brien Trophy*. It is the ultimate symbol of team success. The Larry O'Brien Trophy, named after the former NBA Commissioner, is given to the team that wins the NBA championship.

Winning the Larry O'Brien Trophy is not an easy task. It is a long road from October to June when the NBA Finals end. Teams play a preseason schedule, plus 82 games during the regular season, and if the team has a winning record, then it advances to the NBA playoffs.

So, what does it take for a team to win the NBA's ultimate prize? For starters, talent, health, hard work, teamwork plus a sprinkle of luck along the way.

The NBA began awarding the championship trophy going way back to 1946-47. That's more than 60 years ago! The league was a lot smaller than it is today. There were 11 teams in the NBA's first season. Teams were located in such cities as Boston, New

1946-47 Philadelphia Warriors

York, and Philadelphia, and in the Midwest, Chicago, Detroit, and Cleveland.

The Philadelphia Warriors were the first NBA team to win the league's first championship. The Warriors defeated the Chicago Stags in five games. There wasn't any television coverage or Internet when those games were played. You were lucky if you were able to hear the games on the radio. If you weren't able to get a ticket to watch in person, then you had to read about it in the newspaper the next day.

Today, the NBA Finals are televised in more than 200 countries all over the world! Fans can watch the games so many different ways. They can sit in front of the television, or go on the Internet and follow the game with updated statistics and instant highlights. All the information about the games today is at your fingertips.

So what does winning an NBA championship mean for a team and its players? It means everything. Teams that win championships are forever remembered in the history books. Winning an NBA championship is a goal for all players because it is a team accomplishment, not an individual award. There are plenty of great NBA players who have won all sorts of individual awards such as MVPs and earned All-Star appearances, who would trade them all in just for one NBA title.

Every player who puts on an NBA uniform understands that the ultimate measure of greatness is defined by championships.

1953-54 Lakers

Kareem Abdul-Jabbar, 1982 NBA Finals

Bill Russell & Red Auerbach

CHAPTER 2

DYNASTIES

What is a dynasty? A dynasty represents dominance. A team that is so great that it wins multiple championships in a short period of time. Since the NBA began in 1946-47, the league has featured several teams that have dominated the competition. Here are the NBA's dynasties that have made a lasting mark.

Michael Jordan, 1998 NBA Finals

Tim Duncan & David Robinson, 2003 NBA Finals

George Mikan

Slater Ma

Jim Pollard

Minneapolis Lakers (1949-50, 1952-54)

The Minneapolis Lakers were the NBA's first dynasty. Led by the league's first superstar, George Mikan, the Lakers won five titles in six seasons (1948-49 through 1953-54). Mikan was dominant, winning five straight scoring titles. At 6'10", opposing teams couldn't stop him. Mikan could score with either hand and always put himself in great position, right under the basket. Mikan was so great that the NBA changed the rules to give other players and teams a chance against the Lakers. The league widened the lane under the basket from six feet to 12 feet. Even with the wider lane, teams still couldn't stop Mikan from getting close to the basket. He still scored whenever he wanted.

As great as Mikan was, though, the Lakers were not a one-man show. The team featured other great players. Slater Martin, a scrappy point guard, played a key role in making the Lakers go. In addition to Mikan, the forward positions featured Jim Pollard, a smooth player who was able to hit the jump shot with ease, and Vern Mikkelsen, who used his size and strength to overpower his opponents.

John Kundla served as the head coach of the Lakers. Under Kundla, the Lakers were well-disciplined and played great defense. Kundla not only knew the Xs and Os, but also knew how to work with his players.

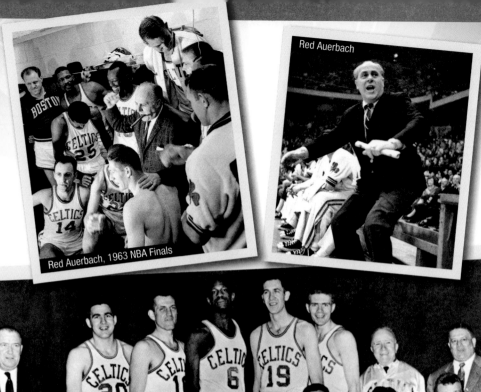

Red Auerbach, 1963 NBA Finals

Red Auerbach

1957 Boston Celtics

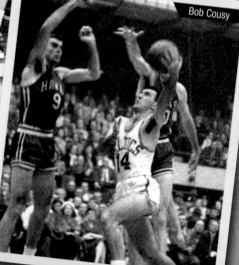

Bob Cousy

Boston Celtics (1957, 1959-66, 1968-69)

It is the greatest dynasty in NBA history. The Boston Celtics won 11 titles in 13 seasons, including eight in a row! The mastermind of the Celtics was Red Auerbach, who served as both head coach and general manager. Auerbach, the general manager, knew what kind of players Auerbach, the coach, wanted.

In April 1956, Auerbach acquired three future Hall of Famers — Bill Russell, Tom Heinsohn, and K.C. Jones — through the NBA Draft and trade. Russell, Heinsohn, and Jones played key roles in the Celtics' success.

Russell was the ultimate team player who was also the league's top defender. Russell ran the floor with great speed, blocked shots, grabbed rebounds, and was always one step ahead of his opponent. Russell proved that defense wins championships.

From Russell's rookie season (1956-57) through his last season (1968-69) the Celtics won the NBA title in every season except two. Russell is the only player in NBA history with 11 championship rings.

Other great Celtics include Bob Cousy, Sam Jones, K.C. Jones, Bill Sharman, John Havlicek, and Satch Sanders.

The Celtics were all about team. To this day, no Celtic has ever led the league in scoring.

Los Angeles Lakers (1980, 82, 85, 87-88)

Five titles in nine years, that was the mark the Lakers left on the 1980s. Led by one of the greatest centers in NBA history — Kareem Abdul-Jabbar — and one of the greatest all-around players the game has seen: 6'9" point guard Magic Johnson. Thanks to Johnson and Abdul-Jabbar, the Lakers were off and running.

"Showtime" was what they called the style of play in Los Angeles. Up-tempo, lightening quick, Magic led the Lakers on their famous fastbreak. It was a beautiful style of play that thrilled fans not just on the West Coast, but all over the world!

Magic made sure all of his teammates — Abdul-Jabbar, Byron Scott, James Worthy, and Bob McAdoo — were involved in the offense. Head coach Pat Riley, a former Laker himself, coached L.A. to four of the five titles in the '80s.

Kareem Abdul-Jabbar & Pat Rile

Kareem Abdul-Jabbar

Magic Johnson, 1987 NBA MVP

Magic Johnson

James Worthy

Michael Jordan

Dennis Rodman

Scottie Pippen

John Paxson

Chicago Bulls (1991-93, 1996-98)

It took Michael Jordan seven years to win his first NBA title. After that, he and the Chicago Bulls won championships in bunches. Jordan led the Bulls to three consecutive titles in the early '90s (1991-93). Jordan retired in '93 and returned to the NBA a year and a half later, ready for more championships.

The Bulls won three more NBA titles in a row (1996-98) for a total of six in eight years.

Even though Jordan won the Finals MVP Award during each of those championships, he couldn't have accomplished his championship goal without the help of his teammates. Jordan counted on his teammates — Scottie Pippen, Horace Grant, Bill Cartwright, John Paxson, and Dennis Rodman — to win.

Los Angeles Lakers (2000-02)

Three titles in a row. The Lakers were peaking at the turn of the 21st Century, winning championships from 2000-2002. Shaquille O'Neal, the 7'1" center, led the Lakers to historical greatness. O'Neal won three consecutive titles and also had the support of All-Star Kobe Bryant.

While O'Neal and Bryant headlined the Lakers championship teams, it was total team effort that was needed for championship success.

Robert Horry, Derek Fisher, and Rick Fox all played huge roles on the team. Phil Jackson, the former head coach of the Bulls, made a championship difference in Los Angeles. Jackson led the Lakers to its first title since 1988.

Kobe Bryant & Shaquille O'Neal

Derek Fisher & Rick Fox

Shaquille O'Neal

Kobe Bryant

Tim Duncan

Manu Ginobili

Tony Parker

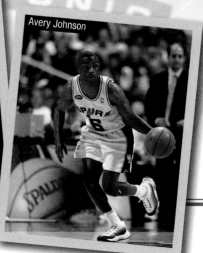

Avery Johnson

Robert Horry

San Antonio Spurs

(1999, 2003, 2005, 2007)

Four NBA titles in nine years. The San Antonio Spurs ruled the NBA in 1999, 2003, 2005, and 2007. The mark of a great team is to be able to win championships with different players. The Spurs won its first title in 1999 and only one player remained on the roster from that title team in 2007.

There were two constants in the Spurs success. One was Tim Duncan, a supremely gifted power forward who could also play center. Duncan won three Finals MVP Awards. The other was head coach Gregg Popovich, who coached all four championship teams.

Although there were many other players who contributed to the team's success, the Spurs won thanks to great contributions from players such as Avery Johnson, Sean Elliott, Robert Horry, Manu Ginobili, and Tony Parker.

GREAT CHAMPIONSHIP GAMES

There have been many great championship games over the years. Actually so many that you can devote an entire book on great championship games. Here are some that really stood out.

Cousy Dribbles Out the Clock
(Boston Celtics 110, Los Angeles Lakers 107, OT, April 18, 1962)

After Frank Selvy missed a game-winning shot for the Lakers at the end of regulation, the Celtics ended up winning, 110-107, in OT. Bill Russell had 30 points and 40 rebounds, and Bob Cousy famously dribbled around the backcourt with a clock-burning display of right-handed ball-handling.

Bill Russell

Bob Cousy

West's Wing and A Prayer
(New York Knicks 111, Los Angeles Lakers 108, OT, April 29, 1970)

The moment occurred in an era, which predated the three-point shot, yet will always live among the greatest Finals games (and calls) in NBA history.

"West throws it up! He makes it! West threw it up and makes it!" shouted New York Knicks announcer Bob Wolff.

Jerry West's desperation 60-foot shot swished through the net, amazingly tying Game 3 between the visiting New York Knicks and Los Angeles Lakers at 102. It was a miraculous shot, given the circumstances and what little time West had to work with after Knicks forward Dave DeBusschere made a driving layup to give New York a 102-100 lead. Laker center Wilt Chamberlain inbounded the ball and West took it from there, racing up the court, dribbling three times before letting it fly 10 feet beyond half court. *Swish!*

DeBusschere collapsed in pure disgust while the Lakers celebrated, some more than others such as Chamberlain, who ran off the court thinking the Lakers were victorious. Unfortunately for West and the Lakers, the NBA didn't adopt the ABA three-point rule until nine years later.

Despite the shocking turn of events for New York, swingman Dick Barnett wasn't about to allow his

Jerry West

teammates to feel sorry for themselves as the game headed into the extra session: "What's the matter with you guys?" asked Barnett. "This game's not over. It's just starting."

Barnett played a key role in New York's overtime victory, hitting the game winner with four seconds remaining as the Knicks defeated the Lakers, 111-108, to take a 2-1 series lead.

Greatest Game Ever?
(Boston Celtics 128, Phoenix Suns 126, 3OT, June 4, 1976)

The Celtics rolled into the NBA Finals as the heavy favorite over the 42-40 Phoenix Suns, who came in off a series of playoff upsets. With the series even at two games apiece, little did anyone anticipate the drama about to unfold in Game 5 at the Boston Garden.

Jump ahead to the second overtime in which the Suns appeared to have won the game, 110-109. Except John Havlicek of the Celtics had other plans as he hit a leaning bank shot. Celtics 111, Suns 110.

One second remained on the clock. After Phoenix called a timeout it didn't have, the Celtics shot a free throw. The Suns inbounded the ball and a basketball miracle happened. Gar Heard hit a turnaround shot with no time left on the clock.

"Gar Heard turnaround shot in the air . . . AAAAAHHHHHH," yelled announcer Brent Musburger. *"IT'S GOOD!! IT'S TIED AGAIN! I DON'T BELIEVE IT!!!"*

The Suns did it once again! Triple overtime.

In the third OT, the Celtics rode deep reserve Glenn McDonald to a six-point lead with 36 seconds remaining. But the Suns didn't fade as a pair of free throws by Westphal ultimately cut the deficit to 128-126.

It was in the remaining seconds where Westphal nearly made yet another steal, only to have Joseph White beat him to the ball. Final: Celtics 128, Suns 126 (3 OT).

John Havlicek

Gerald Henderson

Henderson Steals One from the Lakers
(Boston Celtics 124, Los Angeles Lakers 121 (OT), May 31, 1984)

It was desperation time at the Garden as the Celtics trailed, 113-111, with 18 seconds remaining and the prospect of heading to Los Angeles down 0-2 appearing very much real. With Magic Johnson inbounding the ball to James Worthy and the Lakers looking to run out the clock, it was Gerald Henderson who provided the Garden heroics.

Henderson swooped in, picked off Worthy's soft crosscourt pass to Byron Scott and easily drove in for the layup, tying the game and forcing overtime.

In OT, Henderson once again made a key play, this time finding Scott Wedman on the baseline for a jumper to help the Celtics preserve a come-from-behind victory.

MJ Seals Title Number Six for Chicago
(Chicago Bulls 87, Utah Jazz 86, June 14, 1998)

With the Chicago Bulls trailing by three points in the final minute, Michael Jordan did was he does best — take over a game. Jordan first scored on a drive, and then he stripped the ball from Karl Malone at the defensive end. That set up one of the Finals' greatest performances of all time. With the game clock running down, Jordan hit the game-winning shot, a 20-footer with 5.2 seconds left, that gave the Bulls an amazing 87-86 victory and their sixth championship in eight years.

Jordan finished the game with 45 points and won his sixth Finals Most Valuable Player Award.

Michael Jordan

Wade a Comeback!
(Miami Heat 98, Dallas Mavericks 96, June 13, 2006)

After losing Games 1 and 2 by an average of 12 points in Dallas, the Heat were well aware that no team in Finals history had ever come back from an 0-3 deficit and won an NBA title.

Trailing by 13 with 6:34 remaining and the Miami crowd growing increasingly frustrated, Dwyane Wade singlehandedly willed the Heat back into the game and series, igniting a breathtaking 12-2 run. Wade was unstoppable despite a sore left knee — bank shot, jump shot, slashes to the basket — scoring nine points during the stretch.

What Wade did was everything as the sellout crowd sprung to life, tasting victory as the Heat suddenly surged ahead, 95-93, thanks, in large part, to clutch free throw shooting by Shaquille O'Neal and Udonis Haslem.

While the Heat was white-hot down the stretch, the Mavs were ice-cold, going scoreless for nearly five minutes until Devin Harris tied the game with a driving layup with 33.5 seconds remaining. Miami surged ahead as Gary Payton picked the most opportune time to drain his only field goal of the game, a 16-foot jumper from the right side at the 9.3-second mark.

The Heat's comeback from 13 down in the fourth

Dwyane Wade

was the largest in Finals play since the Chicago Bulls trailed by 15 to the Portland Trail Blazers during the fourth quarter of Game 6 in the 1992 Finals before winning 97-93.

"The basketball gods were good to us tonight," said Miami head coach Pat Riley after the game.

Tim Duncan & David Robinson

Bill Russell & Red Auerbach

Larry B

Kobe Bryant & Shaquille O'Neal

NBA CHAMPIONSHIP GAMES
(YEAR BY YEAR)

NBA Championship Teams		Finals MVP
2008-09	Los Angeles Lakers, Orlando Magic 4-1	**Kobe Bryant,** Los Angeles
2007-08	Boston Celtics, Los Angeles Lakers 4-2	**Paul Pierce,** Boston
2006-07	San Antonio, Spurs Cleveland Cavaliers 4-0	**Tony Parker,** San Antonio
2005-06	Miami Heat, Dallas Mavericks 4-2	**Dwyane Wade,** Miami Heat
2004-05	San Antonio Spurs, Detroit Pistons 4-3	**Tim Duncan,** San Antonio
2003-04	Detroit Pistons, Los Angeles Lakers 4-1	**Chauncey Billups,** Detroit Pistons
2002-03	San Antonio Spurs, New Jersey Nets 4-2	**Tim Duncan,** San Antonio
2001-02	Los Angeles Lakers, New Jersey Nets 4-0	**Shaquille O'Neal,** Los Angeles
2000-01	Los Angeles Lakers, Philadelphia 76ers 4-1	**Shaquille O'Neal,** Los Angeles
1999-00	Los Angeles Lakers, Indiana Pacers 4-2	**Shaquille O'Neal,** Los Angeles
1998-99	San Antonio Spurs, New York Knicks 4-1	**Tim Duncan,** San Antonio
1997-98	Chicago Bulls, Utah Jazz 4-2	**Michael Jordan,** Chicago
1996-97	Chicago Bulls, Utah Jazz 4-2	**Michael Jordan,** Chicago
1995-96	Chicago Bulls, Seattle SuperSonics 4-2	**Michael Jordan,** Chicago
1994-95	Houston Rockets, Orlando Magic 4-0	**Hakeem Olajuwon,** Houston
1993-94	Houston Rockets, New York Knicks 4-3	**Hakeem Olajuwon,** Houston
1992-93	Chicago Bulls, Phoenix Suns 4-2	**Michael Jordan,** Chicago
1991-92	Chicago Bulls, Portland Trail Blazers 4-2	**Michael Jordan,** Chicago
1990-91	Chicago Bulls, Los Angeles Lakers 4-1	**Michael Jordan,** Chicago
1989-90	Detroit Pistons, Portland Trail Blazers 4-1	**Isiah Thomas,** Detroit
1988-89	Detroit Pistons, Los Angeles Lakers 4-0	**Joe Dumars,** Detroit
1987-88	Los Angeles Lakers, Detroit Pistons 4-3	**James Worthy,** Los Angeles
1986-87	Los Angeles Lakers, Boston Celtics 4-2	**Magic Johnson,** Los Angeles
1985-86	Boston Celtics, Houston Rockets 4-2	**Larry Bird,** Boston
1984-85	Los Angeles Lakers, Boston Celtics 4-2	**Kareem Abdul-Jabbar,** Los Angeles

Year	Champions	Finals MVP
1983-84	Boston Celtics, Los Angeles Lakers 4-3	**Larry Bird,** Boston
1982-83	Philadelphia 76ers, Los Angeles Lakers 4-0	**Moses Malone,** Philadelphia
1981-82	Los Angeles Lakers, Philadelphia 76ers 4-2	**Magic Johnson,** Los Angeles
1980-81	Boston Celtics, Houston Rockets 4-2	**Cedric Maxwell,** Boston
1979-80	Los Angeles Lakers, Philadelphia 76ers 4-2	**Magic Johnson,** Los Angeles
1978-79	Seattle SuperSonics, Washington Bullets 4-1	**Dennis Johnson,** Seattle
1977-78	Washington Bullets, Seattle SuperSonics 4-3	**Wes Unseld,** Washington
1976-77	Portland Trail Blazers, Philadelphia 76ers 4-2	**Bill Walton,** Portland
1975-76	Boston Celtics, Phoenix Suns 4-2	**Jo Jo White,** Boston
1974-75	Golden State Warriors, Washington Bullets 4-0	**Rick Barry,** Golden State
1973-74	Boston Celtics, Milwaukee Bucks 4-3	**John Havlicek,** Boston
1972-73	New York Knicks, Los Angeles Lakers 4-1	**Willis Reed,** New York
1971-72	Los Angeles Lakers, New York Knicks 4-1	**Wilt Chamberlain,** Los Angeles
1970-71	Milwaukee Bucks, Baltimore Bullets 4-0	**Kareem Abdul-Jabbar,** Milwaukee
1969-70	New York Knicks, Los Angeles Lakers 4-3	**Willis Reed,** New York
1968-69	Boston Celtics, Los Angeles Lakers 4-3	**Jerry West,** Los Angeles
1967-68	Boston Celtics, Los Angeles Lakers 4-2	*
1966-67	Philadelphia 76ers, San Francisco Warriors 4-2	*
1965-66	Boston Celtics, Los Angeles Lakers 4-3	*
1964-65	Boston Celtics, Los Angeles Lakers 4-1	*
1963-64	Boston Celtics, San Francisco Warriors 4-1	*
1962-63	Boston Celtics, Los Angeles Lakers 4-2	*
1961-62	Boston Celtics, Los Angeles Lakers 4-3	*
1960-61	Boston Celtics, St. Louis Hawks 4-1	*
1959-60	Boston Celtics, St. Louis Hawks 4-3	*
1958-59	Boston Celtics, Minneapolis Lakers 4-0	*
1957-58	St. Louis Hawks, Boston Celtics 4-2	*
1956-57	Boston Celtics, St. Louis Hawks 4-3	*
1955-56	Philadelphia Warriors, Fort Wayne Pistons 4-1	*
1954-55	Syracuse Nationals, Fort Wayne Pistons 4-3	*
1953-54	Minneapolis Lakers, Syracuse Nationals 4-3	*
1952-53	Minneapolis Lakers, New York Knicks 4-1	*
1951-52	Minneapolis Lakers, New York Knicks 4-3	*
1950-51	Rochester Royals, New York Knicks 4-3	*
1949-50	Minneapolis Lakers, Syracuse Nationals 4-2	*
1948-49	Minneapolis Lakers, Washington Capitols 4-2	*
1947-48	Baltimore Bullets, Philadelphia Warriors 4-2	*
1946-47	Philadelphia Warriors, Chicago Stags 4-1	*

* The NBA Finals MVP Award was first issued in 1969